YOUR HEART

By Cyril Bassington

Gareth Stevens
PUBLISHING

Please visit our website, www.garethstevens.com. For a free color catalog of all our high-quality books, call toll free 1-800-542-2595 or fax 1-877-542-2596.

Library of Congress Cataloging-in-Publication Data

Bassington, Cyril, author.
 Your heart / Cyril Bassington.
    pages cm. — (Know your body)
 Includes bibliographical references and index.
 ISBN 978-1-4824-4455-1 (pbk.)
 ISBN 978-1-4824-4399-8 (6 pack)
 ISBN 978-1-4824-4438-4 (library binding)
 1. Heart—Juvenile literature. 2. Cardiovascular system—Juvenile literature. 3. Human physiology—Juvenile literature. I. Title.
 QP111.6.B37 2017
 612.1'7—dc23

                              2015021477

Published in 2017 by
Gareth Stevens Publishing
111 East 14th Street, Suite 349
New York, NY 10003

Copyright © 2017 Gareth Stevens Publishing

Designer: Andrea Davison-Bartolotta
Editor: Therese Shea

Photo credits: Cover, p. 1 Rawpixel/Shutterstock.com; pp. 3, 4, 6, 8, 10, 12, 14, 16, 18, 20, 22–24 Anna Frajtova/Shutterstock.com; p. 5 (both) Sebastian Kaulitzki/Shutterstock.com; p. 7 (main) Ron Levine/Getty Images; p. 7 (inset) Liya Graphics/Shutterstock.com; p. 9 Lightspring/Shutterstock.com; p. 11 sciencepics/Shutterstock.com; pp. 13 (inset), 15 (inset) Alila Medical Media/Shutterstock.com; p. 13 (main) Federico Rostagno/Shutterstock.com; p. 15 (main) Siri Stafford/Photodisc/Thinkstock; p. 17 (main) Eraxion/iStock/Thinkstock; p. 17 (inset) Designua/Shutterstock.com; p. 19 busayamol/Shutterstock.com; p. 21 Golden Pixels LLC/Shutterstock.com.

Printed in the United States of America

CPSIA compliance information: Batch #CS16GS: For further information contact Gareth Stevens, New York, New York at 1-800-542-2595.

CONTENTS

Boldface words appear in the glossary.

Pump It!

Your heart is found in your upper chest, a bit to the left. It **pumps** blood around your body, from the tips of your fingers and toes to the top of your head. Blood carries **oxygen** and **nutrients** and takes away waste.

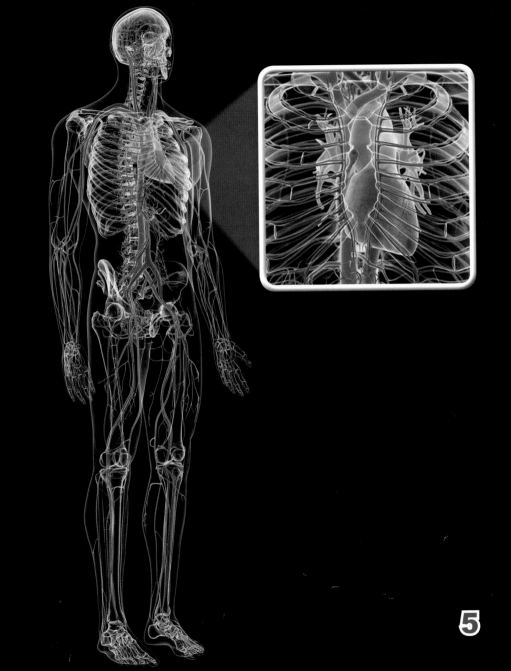

Your heart is made of strong **muscles**. It **squeezes** and **relaxes** to move blood. That's called a heartbeat. Your heart may beat 70 to 110 times per minute! A lot of blood passes through your heart in this time.

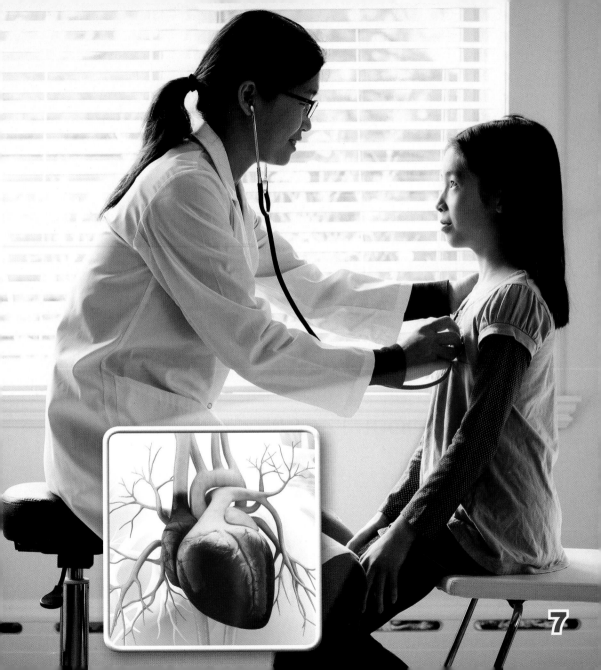

What It Looks Like

Your heart isn't a heart shape. It's more like an upside-down pear. It's a bit larger than your fist. Your heart grows as you do. An adult's heart weighs about 12 ounces (340 g). That's about as heavy as two small apples.

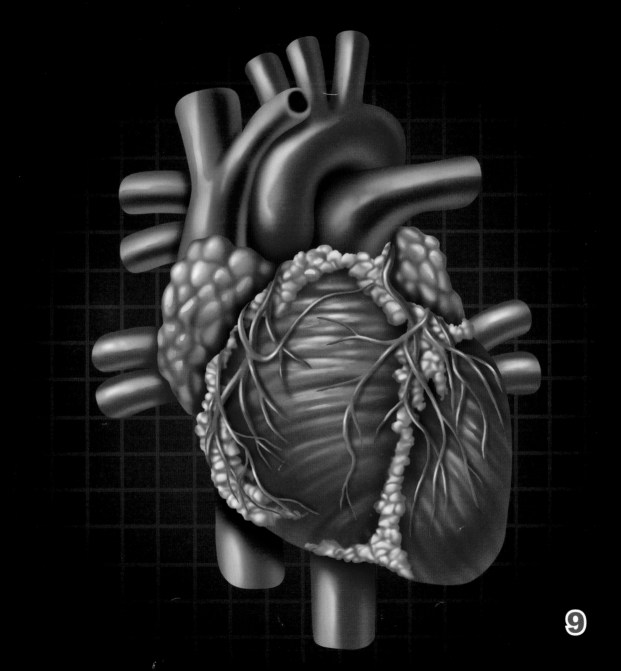

The heart has four parts. The top chambers, or spaces, are called the left atrium (AY-tree-uhm) and right atrium. The lower chambers are called the left ventricle (VEHN-truh-kuhl) and right ventricle. Blood takes a special path through these chambers.

right atrium

left atrium

right ventricle

left ventricle

11

How It Works

Blood from the body flows into the right atrium. It carries a waste gas called carbon dioxide. It then goes into the right ventricle, which pumps it into the lungs. There, blood lets go of carbon dioxide and receives oxygen.

to
right
atrium

to lungs

right
ventricle

13

Next, the left atrium fills with oxygen-rich blood from the lungs. The blood then goes into the left ventricle, which pumps it out into the body. All these movements happen at the same time and in the same direction.

to body

to left atrium

left ventricle

15

The blood circulates, or travels, throughout the body in **blood vessels**. Blood vessels that carry blood away from the heart are called arteries. Blood vessels that carry blood back to the heart are called veins.

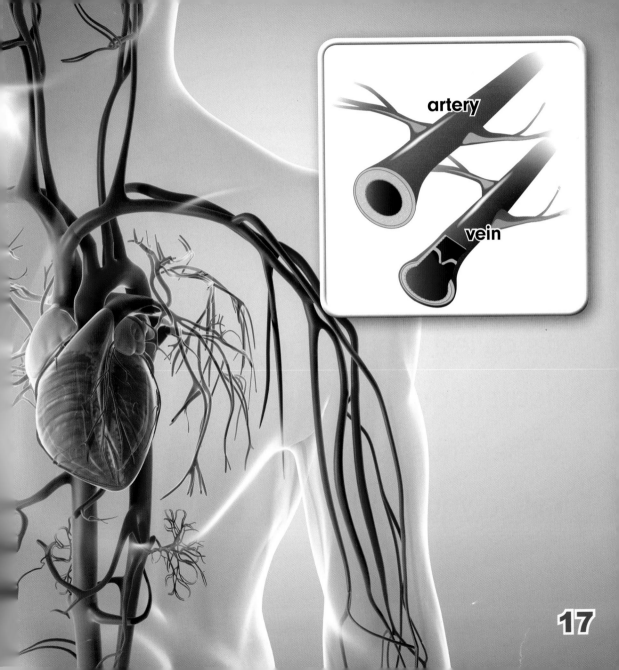

artery

vein

Heart Healthy

Put your fingers on the inside of your wrist. Do you feel that beat? It's called a pulse, and it's your heart in action. It takes about 60 seconds to pump blood to every **cell** in your body!

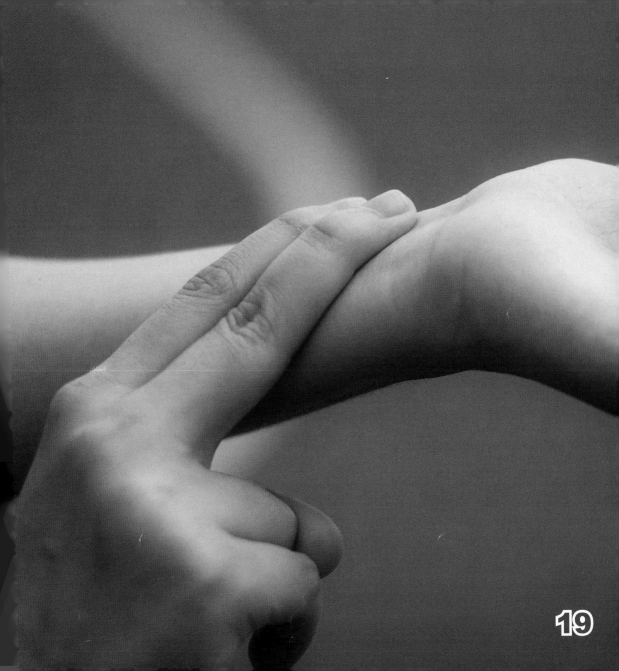

19

Every cell in your body needs oxygen to stay alive. It also needs blood to get rid of waste. Keep your heart healthy by exercising and eating right. Take care of your heart. It takes care of you!

21

GLOSSARY

blood vessel: a small tube in your body that carries blood

cell: the smallest basic part of a living thing

muscle: one of the parts of the body that allow movement

nutrient: something a living thing needs to grow and stay alive

oxygen: a colorless gas you can't smell that many animals, including people, need to breathe

pump: to force a liquid, such as water, through a space

relax: to become looser or less tight

squeeze: to press something tightly

FOR MORE INFORMATION

BOOKS

Bailey, Jacqui. *What Happens When Your Heart Beats?* New York, NY: PowerKids Press, 2009.

Burstein, John. *The Amazing Circulatory System: How Does My Heart Work?* New York, NY: Crabtree Publishing, 2009.

Hewitt, Sally. *My Heart and Lungs.* Laguna Hills, CA: QEB Publishing, 2008.

WEBSITES

Human Heart Facts
www.sciencekids.co.nz/sciencefacts/humanbody/heart.html
Check out more cool heart facts.

Your Heart and Circulatory System
kidshealth.org/kid/htbw/heart.html#
Read more about the blood's path through the heart.

INDEX